Coming to Canada

CAROL SHIELDS

Coming to Canada

CARLETON UNIVERSITY PRESS

Canadian Cataloguing in Publication Data
Shields, Carol, 1935-
    Coming to Canada

Poems.
ISBN 0-88629-186-0 (case)
ISBN 0-88629-187-9 (pbk.)

    I. Title.

PS8587.H46C65 1992 C811'.54 C92-090477-7
PR9199.3.S44C65 1992

Distributed by: Oxford University Press Canada,
70 Wynford Drive,
Don Mills, Ontario,
Canada. M3C 1J9
(416) 441-2941

Front cover art, "Cavan Gothic," acrylic on linen, 39 x 49 inches, 1988, is by John Moffat. Collection of Nicholas Treanor. Special thanks to Dennis Tourbin for helping to locate the image.

Back cover photo of Carol Shields by Jeff de Booy.

Carleton University Press gratefully acknowledges the support extended to its publishing programme by the Canada Council and the Ontario Arts Council, and by the Government of Canada through the Department of Canadian Heritage and the Government of Ontario through the Ministry of Culture, Tourism and Recreation.

Typset in Stempel Garamond
Nancy Poirier Type Services Ltd., Ottawa
Printed in Canada by Love Printing Service Ltd., Ottawa

For Bob and Jane

ACKNOWLEDGEMENTS

The Editor and Carleton University Press would like to thank Borealis Press, Ottawa, for permission to reprint eleven poems from each of *Others* (Borealis Press, 1972) and *Intersect* (Borealis Press, 1974) and the editors of the following magazines in which some of these poems first appeared: *Antigonish Review, Arc, Border Crossings, Canadian Forum, Fiddlehead, Quarry, Salt, The Far Point* and *West Coast Review.*

CONTENTS

Others

INTRODUCTION

While Carol Shields is nowadays widely regarded as being in the forefront of contemporary Canadian fiction writers and is busily developing a second career as a dramatist, few people are familiar with the poetry that made up her first two publications and many are even now unaware that she writes poetry. With fiction so much more visible than poetry in our society this is hardly surprising: in the nineteenth century the same thing happened with Emily Brontë and in our own era we have the examples of D.H. Lawrence and Malcolm Lowry. Even today outside Canada Margaret Atwood is known almost exclusively as a fiction writer. However highly the authors themselves may regard their poetry, it is usually consulted, if at all, only as an aid to the study of their more popular prose work.

In fact, since in Carol Shields' case there are many reciprocal connections, where an acquaintance with the poetry can illuminate or focus aspects of the novels, a brief look at her work in fiction could provide a useful way in to her poetry.

Aside from her M.A. thesis on Susanna Moodie, published in 1977, and her four plays, Carol Shields' major work over the past seventeen years has consisted of seven and a half novels (the half being her share of an epistolary novel, *A Celibate Season*, co-authored with Blanche Howard, that appeared in 1991) and two collections of short stories, *Various Miracles* and *The Orange Fish*.

The first four novels come in matching pairs: *Small Ceremonies*, set in an Eastern Ontario city that later turns out to be Kingston, has as its protagonist and first person narrator, Judith, who, like Shields herself at that time, is working on a study of Susanna Moodie, while its sequel, *The Box Garden,* focuses on a visit to Toronto by Judith's sister, Charleen, a devoted single mother living in Vancouver, who is successful enough as a poet to have had her four volumes re-published in a boxed set. *Happenstance* and *A Fairly Conventional Woman* are set in suburban Chicago where the author herself grew up. Or rather, *Happenstance* employs a male protagonist, Jack, who stays at home with his two teenage children for five days while his wife Brenda, the 'fairly conventional woman', is away at a convention of quilters in Philadelphia, this episode then forming the background of most of the latter novel.

At first sight the fifth novel, *Swann: A Mystery,* seems to mark a departure from this pattern. In one sense it certainly does, for the novel has four protagonists, two male and two female, only one of them narrated in the first person, and all with divergent, indeed clashing, viewpoints. Although they have got to know each other through their correspondence — writing letters is another of Shields' favourite social rituals — they do not actually meet until the symposium, set out in dramatic form, that forms the final section of the novel. Nor are they united through family but through their common quest for the literary remains of the title heroine, Mary Swann, a major but only recently discovered poet, whose work they have all in their different ways and for different motives helped to publicize. However here, as also in her sixth novel, *The Republic of Love* (the only one set in Winnipeg, the city that has been her home for the past thirteen years) the main theme remains that of love, mostly seen in the context of family and marriage and clearly regarded primarily as a redemptive rather than as a destructive force. This domesticated love is felt to be a haven from forces in our society that for the most part affect *other* people. Just as Jack Bowman, the protagonist of *Happenstance*, has trouble imagining the lives of ordinary, unskilled workers, so Carol Shields herself never ventures socio-economically below the level of secretaries.

What has changed in the course of the six novels is the explicit-
ness with which sexual relationships are treated. This is partly a mat-
ter of vocabulary, which has gradually become franker and more
colloquial as Shields tries on other voices perhaps further removed
from her own, though as late as her third novel, *Happenstance*, some
of the physical details of various characters' sex lives have an obliga-
tory feel to them, as if the author were anxious to prove that she too
could handle such scenes. It is also in part due to the wider range of
protagonists, some of whom either never were or are no longer part of
a family unit, and whose sexual, like their social, needs go beyond the
more traditional arrangements of the earlier books. Thus Shields
moves from the self-consciousness of Brenda, the title character of *A
Fairly Conventional Woman* as she considers 'articles about women
who understood and provided for the needs of their bodies, who
took as their due a satisfying schedule of "screwing" — yes, that
was the word for it now; only sweet Mrs. Brenda Bowman from
Elm Park, Illinois, still referred to the act of love as the act of love.
What a dumb sap she was, detained too long in girlhood, an abstainer
from the adult life', to the genuinely funny but barbed account in *The
Republic of Love* of an encounter between the temporarily 'available'
Tom, one of the protagonists, and Charlotte, to whom he has been
introduced by mutual friends and who subjects him to an interroga-
tion before they make love, starting off with:

"We'd better talk about the matter of precautions first,"
she said. She showed him her condoms and he showed her
his. "I hope you don't mind if we use mine," she said. "I'd
feel better."

None of this appears in the poetry.

Nor, for all her considerable ironic gifts, is there any equivalent
in the poetry for the almost set-piece satire that we find in the novels.
Again, however, there are important distinctions to be made.
Sometimes, as in *The Box Garden,* one almost has the sense of a
straw man being attacked, in this case an all-purpose ex-60s hippie,
pretentiously impractical and heavily into meditation. On the other

hand the portrait in the same book of Charleen's mother, narrow, rigid, carping and self-righteous, is brilliant in its vicious accuracy. *Swann* and *The Republic of Love*, by contrast, juxtapose the frequently acerbic viewpoints of the various characters so that we are less aware of an overriding authorial perspective and more of a virtuoso play of ideas, theories and perceptions or of characters unwittingly holding themselves up to ridicule for the pretentiousness of their language or behaviour. Which is not to deny that in lines like Sarah Maloney's in *Swann* '"I love you too", say I, biting into silence as though it were a morsel of blowfish and keeping my fingers crossed' we find ample evidence of the gift for metaphor, for the finely honed phrase, that characterizes most of her poetry.

Such matters of technique and tone aside, however, there remain large areas of common ground in the attitudes behind both poetry and fiction. Part of this is summed up in the title of her first novel, *Small Ceremonies*. Carol Shields is very aware of the social stratagems, the rituals, the habits and expectations that structure fictional entanglements. By comparison with the novels and short stories, the treatment of similar themes in the poetry — school reunions, weddings, putting the clocks forward or back, stacking firewood for the winter — will seem more like snapshots or stills. But by the very fact that such events or ceremonies are singled out for the duration of a short poem rather than, as in the fiction, forming part of a cumulative series of actions, they focus our attention on certain qualities of life, notably the importance of family, the transcendance of enduring, conjugal love, the desirability or normalcy and the value of reticence.

Lest we were in any doubt, the fact that many of the protagonists of these novels are themselves writers of one sort or another — Judith in *Small Ceremonies* is a biographer, Charleen in *The Box Garden* is a poet, Jack in *Happenstance* is a researcher in history, Sarah Maloney is a literary critic — means that Carol Shields has many legitimate occasions on which to suggest her poetic preferences. Charleen, for instance, thinks of the poet's role as reporting on surfaces, while the literary biographer Jimroy in *Swann* distrusts the flashy line and pyrotechnics in poetry: 'It was so easy for a poem to be fraudulent, for what was the difference really between an ellipsis and a vacuum?' So too Fay, in *The Republic of Love*, quotes with approval Leonardo da Vinci's dictum that art lives from constraint and dies from freedom, while elsewhere — in the stories 'Collision' and 'Family Secrets' from *The Orange Fish*, for instance — we find similar praise for the necessity of a certain amount of concealment, even between spouses, and the pointlessness of overt self-revelation. Finally, speaking in her own voice in her study of Susanna Moodie, Carol Shields says, "In order to see Mrs. Moodie in perspective it is important to remember that she was not primarily a writer; she was a Canadian pioneer, a wife and mother who happened also to write. Thus she is reticent and understandably reluctant to sacrifice her position in society by blatant personal declarations."

All this in a sense changes in scale and complexity with Shields' most recent novel, *The Stone Diaries*, in 1993. Short-listed for the Booker Prize and winner not just of the Governor General's Award for Fiction but also of the Pulitzer Prize, this tour de force expands not only the range of her subject-matter but also the versatility and subtlety of her technique. Although crucial parts of the book are located in rural Manitoba and Ottawa, other locales include Florida; Bloomington, Indiana; the Orkney Islands; and London, England. But they are never there simply for local colour: these places, together with the extensive time span of the novel, from 1905 with the birth of her protagonist, Daisy Flett, to the present day, enable Shields to convey something of the full sweep of the century, something that we look for in major novelists, a sense both of the passage of time and of the uniqueness of the times experienced. Gone is that air of willed containment that at times constricted the earlier novels. Indeed, *The Stone Diaries* reveals a slyly unobtrusive architecture that allows an anchoring in details no less firm than before but that, because of the counterpoint, or perhaps the counterpane, the quilt, of seemingly random pieces of evidence, evokes for us a sense of breadth and spaciousness from the letters and diaries quoted and from the casual allusions to incidents or persons whose significance is explained only perhaps sixty pages later. It is almost as if the author had supplied us with part of a jigsaw puzzle and then stood over us as we tried out the various other pieces to see what would fit where. Likewise, the characters, who now come from a far wider range both in social background and in biological age, are allowed to give themselves away without editorial comment, so that we seem to co-operate with them in assembling the narrative. Curiously, although the sequence of chapter headings such as 'Birth, 1905', 'Marriage, 1927' or 'Motherhood, 1947', seems to indicate a straightforward biographical approach, the effect is far more that of a stream-of-consciousness novel. Specifically I was reminded at times of *Mrs Dalloway* since, for all their obvious differences, Daisy Flett shares with Woolf's protagonist the same ongoing sense of isolation, disconnectedness and loneliness in the midst of the world's activities. We come away from the book wiser but sadder.

After *The Stone Diaries* it is no longer possible to think of Carol Shields' work as deriving mainly from areas that we associate with romantic fiction, albeit of the most reserved, Jane Austen-like kind. By the same token, her distancing devices, in her prose no less than in her poetry, preclude any sense of the confessional mode. That still, however, leaves us with a lot of possibilities, many of them in areas of language and theme that have not been a major part of the modern Canadian poetic tradition as represented by such contemporaries as Margaret Atwood, Gwendolyn MacEwen or Phyllis Webb.

* * * * * *

In fact the first thing one is likely to notice about her first book of poetry, *Others*, is the aptness of the title. Most of the poems contained here are indeed evocations of other people, such as 'Our Old Professor', 'An Old Lady We Saw', 'The New Mothers', 'A Friend of Ours Who Knits.' Even in poems like 'A Wife, Forty-five, Remembers Love', where, despite the age discrepancy, we might have suspected some more personal reference, this is held at bay by one of two main stratagems: either it is couched in the third person (or, sometimes, the impersonal 'you'), or Shields retreats behind the collective 'we' that we assume to mean either her husband and herself or her whole family. In only at most seven poems out of fifty-one is there an 'I' speaker and in at least three of those it represents a persona rather than an identifiable aspect of the poet herself. The titles say it all: 'A woman we know suffers from occasional depression', 'What our Toronto friends said' or 'An acquaintance of ours who is an obsessive Christian.' This habit cannot but help imply an oppressively strong and ubiquitous family unit, an impression that is reinforced by an endless repertoire of aunts, grandmas and children. This can easily lead to a sense of stifling coziness. For not only does Shields avoid anything that could be construed as confessional; by remaining so obviously an observer she also deliberately conceals any overtly personal reactions. The focus of observation is strictly on the family, friends, and the neighbourhood — in fact, 'Neighbourhood Watch' could well have served as an overall title for this whole selection.

Such apparently restricted subject matter and the attitudes it usually entails might well have proved debilitatingly trivial were it not for two related qualities that Shields brings to her work: wit and a very sure technical command of cadence and stanza form.

Unlike humour, wit is not one of the most prized qualities in Canadian poetry today, if it ever was. A quality of mind, wit relishes brevity, elegance, conciseness, all attributes that are at odds both with the idea of the Great Canadian Poem that will create a national myth and with much of the poetry of self-exploration of recent feminist poets. Wit implies perspective and distancing and one can think of only a few Canadian poets — P.K. Page, Florence McNeil, D.G. Jones, Pat Lowther, Susan Glickman, Don McKay and Robert Zend, for instance — for whom wit, as distinct from the more blatant forms of irony, is a major element in their work.

But there are of course other, non-Canadian sources and even without the four line poem evoking her by name in *Intersect*, one would have suspected the influence of her great American antecedent, Emily Dickinson, while the contemporary British poet Philip Larkin is likewise almost audible behind many turns of phrase. Sometimes this wit appears as an unexpected but strikingly apt analogy, such as we find in the first two stanzas of 'Anne at the Symphony':

She listens like someone submitting
to surgery;
and at twelve she's quiet
under the knife,

stilled in ether, permitting
an alien clarinet
to scoop out an injury
we can't even imagine.

(The positioning of the line breaks in the first, third and fifth lines, with their momentary suspense and surprise, are part of what I mean by elegance). Sometimes the wit is more a matter of the juxtaposition of images. Thus in 'A Wife, Forty-five, Remembers Love', after two stanzas that evoke a past where love made the couple 'liquor-throated...madhouse fluent', the poem concludes with an image familiar to Ottawans at least, that not only surprises us in terms of sense but also suggests a texture, a naturalness and with it an implication of the subordination of the physical to other aspects of the relationship:

And all our limbs
trailed silent
like lumber,
learning the way.

Often too, as in 'A Physicist We Know', the poem comes alive by virtue of a single metaphor, a single word: 'Even while/ we talk, he abstracts/ himself, making *terrier*/ leaps of speculation/ on the quiet.'

As we know from, for instance, Marvell's famous couplet in 'To his coy mistress',

The grave's a fine and private place
but none, I think, do there embrace

wit can involve not just an intellectual perception of connectedness but also a spiritual poise and one that works just as well with Carol Shields' chosen tools of reticence and understatement as with exaggeration. For indeed Carol Shields rarely raises her voice and only seldom questions — there are only two question marks in the whole volume. Instead, she observes carefully, assembles a series of details, as in 'A Friend of Ours Who Knits' — 'her husband's career is secured/ in cablestitch, and her children, double-ribbed, are/ safe from disease' — then lets the readers draw their own conclusions. For the most part our responses are prompted less by affirmations than by the overtones of images, by line breaks or cadence. And this unobtrusiveness extends also to the stanza forms that, as in this example from 'The New Mothers', while often appearing to be free form, are in fact held together by rhyme or half rhyme:

Nearby
the egg-bald babies lie, stretching
pink like rows of knitting,
insects in cases, and cry
tiny metal tunes,
hairpins scratching
sky.

Here as elsewhere, the imagery serves the same effect; drawn from the everyday familiar settings, it re-inforces the sense of a self-contained world.

To some, involved in issues of peace, feminism or the environment, such a statement might seem damning. Certainly as a poet Carol Shields confines herself to what she knows first hand or has heard from friends. In terms of the quality of life we are left with insights and implications rather than ringing declarations. But what she offers is not quietism: a framework of moral awareness is apparent. Thus, at the end of 'An Old Lady We Saw', who has fallen on the ice, when 'her needlepoint mouth' does not curse the cold, the ice and 'our thinly gathered concern, our clockwork sympathy', she is presented as saying 'the wrong thing, the worst thing, thank you thank you.' So too she brings out the ambivalence of two girls at Halloween who 'hesitate, playing the game/ of inside out, hoping the ghost they meet/ is real, fearing it is, knowing/ it might be.' These are perhaps small scale insights but they are of the kind that, with the benefit of hindsight, we would expect from a writer of stories and novels, for without a grip on such detailed awarenesses the larger truths are likely to remain unspoken or unconvincing.

Carol Shields' second volume, *Intersect*, coming only two years later, in 1974, does not depart appreciably from the themes and techniques of the earlier book. There are still many, arguably too many, poems that confine themselves to the family. At the same time there are several that go beyond these familiar themes to treat, for instance, 'Pioneers, Southeast Ontario', 'Volkswagen', 'Fetus' or 'Rough Riders', this last displaying the local football team at 'huddle time' as 'their bums rough/ out lunatic lily pads/ on the comic green.' The range of feelings has likewise slightly increased: 'January', whose weather is seen as affecting not just the people in the house but also the furniture, expresses whimsical hatred for the dishwasher's 'pure cycles' and its inopportunely 'unending cheerfulness.'

The wit is still there in for instance 'Family Friend Aged Ninety' who turns away from the TV while her eyes turn 'into pre-selected darkness' or in 'Child Learning to Talk', but at times now the imagery takes on an arbitrary quality, as in lines like 'our nerve ends scratch, selfish as hens' or, of bulbs about to be planted, 'dry things, colloquial as onions.'

What is new, however, and it is an aspect that links up with the title sequence, 'Coming to Canada', is that she explores not just the present, the parties, the sick friends, but also at times scenes apparently from her own past in poems such as 'Summertime 1950', 'Home Movies 1962' or 'Our Mother's Friends.'

What she is saying in these poems, as in *Others*, coincides very closely with the territory that she stakes out in her first two novels, while the themes that predominate — love, family, stability, happiness — and the corresponding need to transcend habit and decorum, albeit in such marginal ways as appreciating the drunken singing of a man in the subway — are also the themes that animate the novels.

The title sequence, by contrast, differs from the books less in form and content than in its tone, which has now become more wry and informal, incorporating more direct speech and generally exuding

a greater colloquial ease. Most important of all, as befits an auto-
biographical sequence, the poet is speaking in the first person and tak-
ing the liberty of self-conscious asides, as she does here in 'I/Myself':

> But there I was, three
> years old, swinging on the gate
>
> thinking (theatrical, even then)
> here I am, three years old,
> swinging on the gate.

Consciousness is indeed, as Shields says, a 'bold weed' and it is obvi-
ous from these poems that the emphasis has shifted from others,
however sympathetically observed, to the self, viewed from within.
This brings with it a greater emotional realism. It is not necessarily that
the family portraits of *Others* and *Intersect* were idealized: 'Our Old
Aunt Who Is Now in a Retirement Home', for instance, is shown as
'unglued/ in her closet of brown breath/ and her memories/ tremble
like jellies'. Rather the emphasis in a poem like 'When Grandma
Died — 1942' shifts from the physical other to the effect of the
funeral on the seven-year-old speaker:

> When no one was looking I touched
> her mouth — which had not
> turned to dust
> It was hard and cold
> like pressing in the side
> of a rubber ball
>
> Later I would look at my hand
> and think: a part
> of me has touched dead lips.
> I would grow rich with disgust
> and a little awed
> by my hardness of heart

The other big change, which can be parallelled by what happens in the novels, is that the personal is increasingly tied in, understandably given the period in which Shields grew up, with major world events such as the end of the war in 1945.

Along with this change in focus to the personal comes a greater willingness to express negative views, even though this is still largely implicit, in the form of imagery. Thus at the end of 'Dog Days', which portrays her mother combatting the humid heat, the house is 'unsettled/ by the busyness of swivel fans and cross/ drafts, working through the short, soft night,/ banking coolness enough for another day,/ righteousness for another season.' Occasionally, as in 'Vision', these personal conclusions take the form of generalizations. Thus here Uncle George, 'a red faced man who swore a lot', appears to the widow, then becomes

> the kind of legend that
> takes root in awkward families,
> hauled out on spoiled occasions,
> bringing ease or almost-ease
> stretched tight between disgrace
> and unsprung laughter

At the same time the *leitmotif* of love, so central to her fiction, takes on an avowedly personal significance in a poem like 'Love — Age 20'.

Although the poems in the title section deal in fact not with Canada but with her childhood, adolescence and early womanhood in the U.S., up to the age of twenty-two, they do nevertheless introduce for the first time themes that are to figure prominently in her more recent poems, such as a concern with the effects of time and especially the idea of seasons.

How, then, can we characterize these 'new' poems? Some elements have of course remained constant: there are again poems about family members although now, in 'Journey' for instance, the Uncle Harvey whose grave the family visits is frankly recognized as 'the old goat...the old bastard', a man with a drinking problem who was occasionally violent, while in 'Fortune' one of the children of her 'bad cousin' makes her living as a tarot card reader: in other words, all is not quite as cosy and respectable as it once seemed. But while we still find generic portraits such as that of the 'Sunday Painter', and other poems like 'The Reunion' or 'The Class of '53' that fill in real or imagined gaps in the 'Coming to Canada' sequence, the function of most of these poems is to record *moments* of illumination. This is the case with 'Remembering' where a Sunday morning 'made simple/ and slow by old routines' is redeemed almost miraculously by that 'sudden seizure/ of weather and brimming half hour/ of beaten air/ and afterwards a glaze/ of sunlight brighter than/ you could bear'. Other short, attractive poems lead up to a well-tuned aperçu. So it is with 'Sleeping', about children resisting the treachery of sleep, or 'Getting', which deserves quotation in full for the sake of its elegant neatness:

Getting
older we take
chances
with this useful love

Like skaters turning
and pirouetting
on a winter lake
seen at a distance,

we've been learning
the double trick of balance
and indifference

This is only one of the many later poems that deal with time and its effect on human happiness. Whereas the concern is obvious in, say, 'The Invention of Clocks', 'Quartz' or 'At the Clock Museum', in 'Work' by contrast, where husband and wife are stacking cordwood against the garage for the winter, or in 'Cold Storage', which describes fur coats and stoles being put away for the summer, we find a subtler link with two of Carol Shields' favourite and inter-related themes, themselves both aspects of time, rituals and seasons. The putting up for sale of the family home in 'House', with all its connotations of letting go and moving on, likewise involves on a larger scale the same kind not just of chronological but also of psychological adjustment as we see in 'Daylight Saving' or 'Falling Back', while 'Holiday' provides a chance for another kind of change of pace and scene familiar especially from her short fiction.

The major adjustments, however, are those that go beyond the yearly frame and the specific event to the contours of the life itself. Here we have to recognize that Shields, for all her celebration of happiness, harmony and order, is no less aware than Philip Larkin of the sadness, loneliness and anger that accompany old age. This comes out very clearly in the first stanza of 'Fall':

> This is the time of year when golden-agers
> are taken on buses to view the autumn foliage
> as though the sight or scent of yellowed trees
> will stuff them with beautiful thoughts
> and keep them from knowing —

It is fitting too that the final poem here, 'Season's Greetings', should be so clear-sighted about the ambivalence of Christmas cards, that bring with them not 'knowledge or good cheer or love'

> but an eye blinked
> backward at other richer
> seasons, something more slender
> than truth and more kind
>   or less kind
> than letting go.

Carol Shields' poetry turns out not to be as full of sweetness and light as it might at first glance appear.

At present, in what one trusts is not more than her mid-career, Carol Shields' poetry, though it has kept pace with her fiction, is nowhere near so comprehensive in its range of ostensible subject matter nor indeed does it even now command the range of tone that one finds, especially in the last three works, *Swann*, *The Republic of Love*, and *The Stone Diaries* with their multiple viewpoints and their interlocking mosaics of experience. All the same, there may well be further surprises in store for us in her poetry no less than in her fiction.

For instance, the only body of poems not represented in this selection are those few included in *Swann: A Mystery* and supposed to have been written by the fictitious rural Ontario poet, Mary Swann. Although they were presumably invented *ad hoc* for the purpose of the novel — or was it the other way around? — their merits go well beyond pastiche and indeed indicate another kind of poet that Carol Shields could have become or indeed, should she so wish, might yet become. Since the latter part of *Swann* centres on the fate of various rare missing copies of the fictitious poet's work, would it not be reasonable to expect Carol Shields some time to put the various stanzas that she does quote into context by publishing the whole collection?

More realistically, it is to be hoped that the present volume will at least serve for the time being to illuminate, and find further readers for, this too little known aspect of Carol Shields' many-sided talent.

Christopher Levenson
June 1995

COMING TO CANADA

GETTING BORN

Odd that no one knows how
   it feels to be born,
   whether it's one smooth whistling ride
   down green, ether-muffled air
   or whether the first breath burns
   in the lungs with the redness of flames

My time and place are fixed:
   at least — Chicago 1935
   in the "midst of the depression" — as folks said
   then. The hospital still stands,
   a pyramid of red bricks
   made clumsy by air shafts — only now
   there's a modern wing
   smooth as an office tower

The doctor is dead
   not only dead but erased
   "What was his name anyway? An Irish name,
   wasn't it? — began with an M."

            There's something
   careless about this forgetting
   something dull and humiliating
Well, he died in the war
   probably   a young man with
   smooth hands, a blank face
        paved over
   like a kind of cement

The doctor is dead

    Birth is an improvised procedure
    Coming alive
    just half a ceremony
    composed of breath,
    a clutch at simple air —
impossible
    to do it well

You slipped out like a lump of butter
    my mother said
        her voice
    for once
      choked with merriment
    eyes rolled upward toward the ceiling,
    round, white, young,
      clear
         oh shame

LEARNING TO TALK

There's power in primitive grammars
    yes   no   be quiet
attached to polished stairs
    look out   hard   hurt
and unnamed objects in a narrow room
    get out of the way

When phrases fell like hammers
    on dizzy carpet
when words stuck to chairs
    and tables   never to come apart
when language blew up a new balloon
    almost every day

I/MYSELF

A moment of no importance
but there I was, three
years old, swinging on the gate

thinking (theatrical even then)
here I am, three years old
swinging on the gate

There's no choice
about this. Consciousness is a bold
weed, it grows where it wants,
sees what it wants to see

What it sees is a moment within
a moment, a voice
outside a voice

saying: here I am, three
years old, swinging on the gate

ANOTHER BIRTH

Someone (the face is blurred)
gave me a broad blade of grass,
split it with his thumbnail
and showed me how to hold it

It had to be stretched tight,
held just so in that small
oval new-found space
between the thumbs — then

you blew hard across
the taut green blade until
a whistle, then a wail
like a brass bird
weeping   split
the blue air in
two and my life began

THE RADIO — 1940

Like a varnished bear grown up
it hums by the busy wall
The front (I know) is burled oak
and there's cloth where
the sound comes through

It's a darker world at the back
a village spread on a hill
where the static is hatched
and the lights burn red
and the weather hisses
and pops

The inside of my head
is like this
(I know)
all wires and waiting lights
and people
coughing and playing tricks
and the tubes just warming up

DADDY

Weekdays he rode the L
got swallowed up in
the sweet black heat
of downtown
an office somewhere

evenings
he stood still
as a dead man
on the dry front lawn
holding the garden hose
in soft padded hands

and rescued the spoiled air
with rainbows

of all things

WHEN GRANDMA DIED — 1942

It was hard to be sad
when Grandma died
She was old
and never said much
never: *here's a nickel to spend*
or *come sit on Granny's lap*
At the table she clawed
at her food and coughed up phlegm
and people talked behind her back

Now she was dead
in a satin coffin
wearing a black dress
with lace at the chin and smiling too —

When no one was looking I touched
her mouth — which had not
turned to dust
It was hard and cold
like pressing in the side
of a rubber ball

Later I would look at my hand
and think: a part
of me has touched dead lips.
I would grow rich with disgust
and a little awed
by my hardness of heart

I tried to pretend
it was a gesture of love but
it wasn't. It was a test,
one of the first, one of the easiest,
something I had to do

THE METHODIST JESUS

Little Lord Jesus was a sissy but
We liked him anyway
He was like George Washington
And never told lies — only
Much more important   we knew that.

Big Lord Jesus in the brown gown
And sandals with kids climbing on his lap —
He was nice   but you never forgot
He was going to get nailed to the cross
Right through his hands and feet.

Our heavenly Father sat at a big desk
And could see right into our hearts
Where the swear words were and the lies
And the other things, but if you really truly
Wanted something   you only had to ask.

The Holy Ghost?
It was better not
To think about
The Holy Ghost.

It was the Christ Child we liked best
He was always asleep
And had a round halo like the R.C. Jesus
And a look on his face so sweet
It made you want to cry
He was on our level so to speak
Just a little kid   only holy.

THE FOUR SEASONS

Before the War
    was a simple place
    that we couldn't get back
    to somehow

The War
    was right now
    the newsreels kept our terror
    fresh
    our cousin Arnold with
    the Purple Heart
    was in the loony bin
    Some hero, Uncle Freddy said

The Duration
    was holding your breath
    or treading water for America
    or buying bonds
    if you had the cash
    or just doing your part

After the War
    came peace
    kind of like heaven
    Aunt Violet said
    only with regular-type deaths
    like pneumonia
    or cancer or heart attacks
    or something simple and old-fashioned
    and blameless like falling downstairs.

VISITING AUNT VIOLET

Mornings she woke up early and got
dressed. First she put on the pale pink girdle
with the hose that snapped to her thighs
next, a certain cotton housedress crisp and admirable
She was straight from the Rinso ads or so we thought
(There was a pertness in her collar and in her eyes)

Hers was the buoyant mid-American creed
You can be anything you like,
she told us straight — even President!
(not that we believed this for an instant)
Sometimes when her feelings were hurt she cried
and a fearful redness damaged her Rinso look

What would you have been, given the choice?
We asked her this shortly before she died
(impudent question, considering her age)
Just what I am, just what I am, she said
trembling at the trembling in her voice
swallowed by the pinkness of her rage

LEARNING TO READ

Grass grows on the graves of Dick Jane Sally and Spot
They were boring and middleclass and, worse,
they were stereotypes — there's nothing worse than that.

They were put to death. Spot so lively and housebroken
Dick who never picked on little kids
Solid Jane and Sunny Sally, they were taken

away. It was unhealthy to force
the children-of-America to co-relate
with healthy kids, so of course

they had to go. Now there are second rate
kids with shouting mothers and fathers, and token
yellows and blacks, and folks who are overweight

But Dick Jane Sally and Spot did
one good deed. They opened their round pink
mouths and said what had to be said:

that behind the cipher of ink
lay a permanent unlocked code
that could unmake our stubborn fears and unthink

our unthinkable lot
and make us almost as good
and brave as Dick Jane Sally and Spot

WAKING AND SLEEPING

White net curtains printed
with light
the daily trick
of the sun   calm
and steady like money
newly minted

and in the backyard
just past the standing elms
is heard
everyday   the loud drumming
of possibility

a kind of music
collected like alms
against the coming
of the enemy night

that other realm
which again and again dissolves
in a cunning alchemy
that dyes the curtains dark
as the pelts of wolves

their shining hair, their mouths
press at the window panes, guard
the door, give nothing back
but a gleam of snagged light
faintly remembered
in the shadow of day
a tooth, an eye

EASTER

Everything shone,
polish was everywhere, in the throats
of waxed lilies, on the altar rail,
on top of the roadway after the rain,
and in the eyes of our Catholic cousins
(whom we loved and feared) picking at the glazed
ham and shrieking about the end of Lent
and Our Lady who wept with happiness and —

and now — just when everything seems poised
and about to begin, the machinery fails,

always at the moment
of resurrection it fails

The cousins fall silent, the dinner goes uneaten
grey smoke rises and rolls
across the lens

leaving behind the unanswerable thought:
just what is this for? these threats
of re-enactment? these rattling kilowatts
of light shut up in the brain
preserved in their perfect bottles

their faulty brine?

AUNT ADA

Aunt Ada never went to church
Her head ached or her back
and no wonder

She had the pies to bake
and the wash and the children under
foot and not so much

as a minute to sit and ponder
how she'd earned such
blessings or how to take

the anger from her look
or thunder
from her touch.

No one remembers
Aunt Ada much,
except she stayed home sick

on Sundays, rebuked
God, did her work
and grew a little kinder

THE END OF THE WAR — 1945

There was our mother
on the back porch
waving a meat fork
and crying out the words
unconditional surrender

It happened to be suppertime
when the news came purling
out of the old Philco and
setting her on fire

She forgot to take off her apron
even.   It was the tired
end of a hot day and a wonder
to see her step and lurch
like a crazy woman

If only we'd taken a picture
(we said later) and kept it in a frame —
our mother   dancing across the porch
with her single flashing weapon
uniquely in hand
crying *victory, victory* and hurling
us into the future

ENTRY

Grandpa who died young kept
a diary of sorts which was really
just a record of the weather
or how often he was obliged
to have his roof repaired
or when his taxes went up
or the latest news of City Hall
but once, a Sunday, in the year 1925
he entered a single word: woe

It shimmers uniquely on the ruled page
so small it makes us wonder and squint
but large enough in its inky power
to unsettle his young-manly script
and throw black doubt on other
previous entries: *weather tip-top*
or *gingko on Crescent Ave.*

and even darker doubt
on us
    who seize this word
    woe — eagerly, eagerly,
    making it ours

SNOW

In those days, Mrs. Riordan says
(relaxing over a cup of tea)
we had snow all winter long

Snow was different in those days
(reaching for a butter tart)
over our heads like a kind of dream

Her own father lost half his toes
(a little wouldn't hurt)
while walking home from church

yes and colder to the touch
(I wouldn't mind)
piled around the door like shaving cream

You can't imagine how it was
(well, just a crumb)
those white walls, those blinded houses

those boundless deafened days
(I mustn't, I mustn't)
that paradise

BEING HAPPY — 1949

When Uncle Freddy said
   MODERN ART
You could hear the spit
leaving his parted teeth

and when he said
   FRANKLIN DELANO ROOSEVELT
you felt the full thrust
of his curled back lip

When he said
   SEND THE WOPS BACK HOME
you shrank from the crass
emptiness of undealt
blows and from the redness of his heated
mouth

   Well, someone said,
taking me aside,
he's not a happy man.

     Happiness was not
     what I'd thought —
     a useful monotony
     something you could trust

     It was the lucky pane of glass
     you carried about
     in your head
     It took all your cunning
     just to hang on
     to it

     and underneath
     its smooth surface waited
     a raging cavity
     with no way out

VISION

Driving home from Uncle George's funeral
Aunt Marg saw his face glide white
across the highway, then rise
with a look of sorrow into the trees
— this in a family unvisited by visions.

It was bad enough, everyone said,
that she saw poor Uncle George
(a red-faced man who swore a lot)
but did she have to say so —
and out loud — and so soon after?

Just before he melted into space
he gave Aunt Marg a cloudy wink, softer
than his regular wink but large
enough to say that being dead
was lonely as hell.

Then becoming the kind of legend that
takes root in awkward families,
hauled out on spoiled occasions,
bringing ease or almost-ease
stretched tight between disgrace
and unsprung laughter

DOG DAYS

Dog days, our mother called them
wiping at her damp thighs and staying
in all day with just her slip
on and her nylons rolled round her ankles.

First thing in the morning she was up
shutting the windows, pulling down the blinds
so that the rooms grew dark amber in colour,
filling up with motionless air spiked
by the clink of the ice water bottle
and the whap of her newspaper seeking out flies —
— that same hand so helpless and ineffectual
in temperate times —

All day long she conspired and battled
bringing to satisfaction her dimmed corners,
folding and unfolding them carefully like
a kind of theatre, her face a ticking clock
moving forward, ever forward, to the tidal
hour, seven, seven-thirty, when the windows
could be opened, propped up, and the house unsettled
by the busyness of swivel fans and cross
drafts, working through the short, soft night,
banking coolness enough for another day,
righteousness for another season

AWAY FROM HOME — 1954

The hedges had a leggy look but
the sharp leaves sprang out
greener than those at home

There was something odd about
the light, the way the sun came
up and the way it sank down

People were kinder or not
as kind, making you feel at
home or looking the other way

and coins in your pocket clinked
with a harder sound
but were quickly spent

and you started to think
that what you used to
think might be true

that
everything was different
and the same

LOVE — AGE 20

there's something extravagant
about this   something that says
this illness is temporary
and likely to be cured
at any moment

Metaphors fall too fast
for health   scenery bleeds mad music
and the landscape tilts and sways
with the simple sayings of
men and women

and mostly
we're kinder than we thought
possible   breathing please
and thank you like children
who are bewitched
and taking turns and worrying that
this is going to be costly
in the end

But in the end
    in the slow unfolded history
    of our own green
    earth   winking with capsized
    promise and spilt panic —
    this was the only
    thing that would last

    an unearned gift of
    love   which we have
    not trusted or deserved
    or sufficiently praised

    but which
    despite ourselves
    has endured

GIFTS

First there was elderly Uncle George pressing nickels
                                    in our hands
and pointing across the street to the candy store
which left us grateful but uncertain about the shock of
this conversion — coinage into candy — with
no thought of saving or what money was for —
nothing but a stripped and heedless spending

Then there was a young man running in
a crowded street (which could be anywhere). His fine
face was alight with secrecy and he held aloft
a bunch of yellow flowers and as he ran
people stepped aside — willingly — to let him
pass, since what he carried was most certainly a gift

I think: what we could do with three days of
fine weather, how we would hold nothing
back, using it all, every hour on love
beginning with that primal gesture — an open hand that
bears an offering, a gift held briefly (as gifts are)
half in one hand, half in another

COMING TO CANADA — AGE TWENTY-TWO

The postcard said: COME BACK SOON
There was a mountain, a faded lake
with a waterfall and a brown
sun setting in a tan sky

Aunt Violet's Canadian honeymoon
1932   It was swell and she
always meant to go back
but her life got in the way

It was cool and quiet there
with a king and queen
and people drinking tea
and being polite and clean
snow coming down
everywhere

   It took years to happen:
   for the lake to fill up with snow
   for the mountain to disappear
   for the sun to go down

   and years before COME
   BACK SOON changed to
   here and now and home
   the place I came to
   the place I was from

OTHERS

THE NEW MOTHERS

Nearly seven,
walls loosen, it's already dark,
dinner trays rattle by,
nurses slack off, catch
a smoke, let go.
Roses bloom in every room.

Nearby
the egg-bald babies lie, stretching
pink like rows of knitting,
insects in cases, and cry
tiny metal tunes,
hairpins scratching
sky.

The mothers gather
together in clutches
of happy nylon,
brushing and brushing their hair.

They bunch at the frosted windows
in quilted trios
watching the parking lot where

pair after pair
the yellow headlights arc
through blowing snow —
the fathers
      are coming.

JOHN

My young son
eating his lunch, heard a plane go
overhead, and put down his spoon
remarking: the pilot doesn't know

I'm eating an egg. He seemed shocked,
just as if he'd never known
nor suspected he was locked
in, from the beginning, alone.

ANNE AT THE SYMPHONY

She listens like someone submitting
to surgery;
and at twelve she's quiet
under the knife,

stilled in ether, permitting
an alien clarinet
to scoop out an injury
we can't even imagine.

Jittery violins
devise a cure
and the vinegar pure
flutes doodle a theory
of life

which dissolves in
a memory of a memory
and bleeds like sand
through her faintly
clapping hands.

ADVICE FROM A GREEN-THUMBED FRIEND

Slick as waxed water
this rubber plant
swallows up sun,
juicing its green breadth
in a pool of perfect light.

    Disregard its gross health,
    its porous good nature.
    Removed from this graced
    spot it would die in a matter
    of hours, its moist tongues
    torn out.

But watch the philodendron,
tendrilled beyond belief, sprout
precocious from a stringy throat,
insolent with bright
unnecessary growth.

    It out-snakes the future.
    It knows what it wants,
    root-room, leaf volume,
    space, it dreams of jungle space.

AN OLD LADY WE SAW

Before the ambulance came we covered
her with coats since it was cold
on the ice where she fell

and frightening the way her hip
shot out surrealistically.

We saw her slip,
watched her go
down, heard the old
bones crack clean like a bell

She should have cursed
the deceitful ice, the murderous cold,
not to mention our thinly gathered
concern, our clockwork sympathy.

Instead her needlepoint mouth moved, blue
against the oatmeal snow,
saying the wrong thing, the worst
thing, thank you, thank you.

OUR OLD AUNT
WHO IS NOW IN A RETIREMENT HOME

Blinds shut out the bothering sun
    where Auntie lies, stewed
    in authentic age.

She has come unglued
    in her closet of brown breath
    and her memories
    tremble like jellies

There's little to say.
    Awake
    she lives from tray to tray,
    briefly fingering
    squares of cake.

The final outrage
    not death,
    but lingering
    has begun.

THE STOCKING MAN

In the cheap chain store
the man
behind the hosiery counter stands
beneath fluorescent tubes
where futuristic nylon things are sold.

He is an accident in ladieswear,
bull-necked, muscle-ribbed, old,
slow shuffling, confused,
prehistoric behind the crystal cubes.

His language is effete and foreign,
(lock-stitch, fall-shade, easycare.)

He is extinct and knows it, abused
by the young-pup manager,
as hugely helpless
as a dinosaur. His hand
coarse, hairy and
speckled, spreads beneath a stocking
pleading sheerness
and something
more.

OUR OLD PROFESSOR

Our old professor, a thorough man,
stunned a frog with an ether cloud
and stretched its foot on the stand
of a microscope,
    then allowed
us each to look in the miniature ring
at the snarl of thumping veins,

and never knew that the sight and shock
of blood cells moving slick as trains
along a track, unlocked
for a shuttered instant
the secret to everything.

A FRIEND OF OURS WHO KNITS

You'll see her always through a whir
of knitting needles, obscured
by her jigging wool.
She more than keeps
time; this is her way
of swimming to safety.

Odd, or perhaps not so odd,
for in the Newtonian universe
energy is energy
and who's to say
what power is hers.

The mittens that leap
from her anxious wool annul
old injuries and rehearse
her future tense.

Her husband's career is secured
in cablestitch, and her children, double-ribbed, are
safe from disease.

knit, purl,
she goes faster and faster.
increase, decrease,
now she prevents
storms, earthquakes, world wars.

And limb by limb, row by positive row
she is reviving God.

A PHYSICIST WE KNOW

Even while
we talk, he abstracts
himself, making terrier
leaps of speculation
on the quiet.

His smile
is detached and social,
disenfranchised by
his secret alphabet
of air.

Occasionally
he emerges in fractions,
lopsided with camaraderie,
looking rather
hysterical
and frantic.

Then we see him sympathetically
as an exile
and don't dare
ask, is it lonely in there?

A WIFE, FORTY-FIVE,
REMEMBERS LOVE

In those days
love made us liquor
throated, made us
madhouse fluent,

we stacked up stanzas
fat enough for a feast,
puffed hymns
all day, poured
words pentecostal for
forty nights at least.

And all our limbs
trailed silent
like lumber,
learning the way.

INTERSECT

PIONEERS: SOUTHEAST ONTARIO

They existed.   Butter bowls
and hayrakes testify,
and ruined cabins
their grievous roofs
caved in.

But they're melting to myth,
every year harder to believe in,
and the further we travel away
the more we require
in the form of proofs.

Of course
you still meet those who
are old enough to
claim kinship, but eye
witnesses are scarce
now and unreliable.

We want sealers, cutlery, clods
of earth, flames from their fires,
footsteps, echoes, the breath
they breathed,
a sign, something to
keep faith by
before they go the way
of the older gods.

SERVICE CALL

His van arrived
witty as a rooster —
he had come to repair
our troubled telephone

From the window
we watched him race
leather-haunched up
the serious pole

And there —
leaning alone
into green-wired leaves
buzzing with gossip

he phoned from an oval
of space
pure perfect numbers
we'll never know

ROUGH RIDERS

Jogging into view supersized
in wired shoulders and thighs
attached like meat, the least
of them intent on murder,

though they surprise
us by being obedient to whistles,
lining up in tidy rows
more like goodly country lads
than contract heroes.

Huddle-time and their bums rough
out lunatic lily pads
on the comic green.

                                    It's here
that they play at priests
locked in holy circles
plotting death
by numbers
so intricate we're glad
we came after all.

Furthermore, by sitting here
we hold the seasons still.
The sun is a striped beast,
the air just sharp enough
filling the bottom of every breath
with the rasp of winter.

RADIO ANNOUNCER

His throat is a piece of sculpture
designed for ultimate resonance.
His larynx serves the pure
mid-atlantic vibration,
vowels rolling in like vitamins
cut short by the sure
german-chop of consonants

but tasteful tasteful
pitched to avoid offense,
a public masculine
without past or future.

Though it must have been half-
sized once,
a child's voice, shrill
as a whistle.
It might have been
happy, it might even
have laughed

before it vanished
forever inside the great
humming tubes of the varnished
Philco where existence
begins at the station break.

OLD MEN

First to come
the disabling treachery
of language

the slow spaced notes
of speech that detach
themselves and words that freeze
up suddenly   so much for wisdom

then the surprised foliage
of age
hoarse phrases that catch
in folded throats

beg your pardon please
if you will please
excuse me allow me permit me
help me forgive me please please

DAUGHTER

We've seen
her pull spoons from empty air,
small scattered notes, absolute
as coinage,

the pewter sound
of her flute
carrying her further and further
away so that often we
lose sight of her
completely.

The rapid rising stairs
of her breath astonish
our house, and the haemorrhage
of silver, netted like fish,
falls on private ground
where we've never really
been.

MOTHER

While we slept our mother
moved furniture

Through dull unfocused
dreams we could hear
the coarse scrape
of chairs and the sharp sound
of her breath easing
the sofa in place, its plush girth
opening fresh wounds
in the wallpaper

In the morning we found
the amazing corners, startled by pure
circuits of light we'd never
seen before, pleasing
elbows of space and new shapes
to fit into   bringing us
closer to rebirth
than we ever
came   in all those years

UNCLE

When he speaks
it is with the privileged
angular paragraphs
of old essays,
his phrases antique
and shapely as jewelry.

But when he laughs
he touches new territory
somewhere sad between
language and breath
just missing the edge
of what he really
means.

BOYS PLAYING CHESS

They'll grow old
   these young boys hunched intent
   over a chess board.

already they have the gestures
   of old men, the hesitation of hands
   hooked in air over castles and pawns
   prefiguring their futures,

each forward thrust and turn
   pre-recorded.
   from here on
   all moves are planned,

and though they can't see or understand
   and would grieve to be told,
   there's nothing left to learn
   now but a fringe of refinement.

PROFESSOR

When he lectured
    words fell out like fruit,
    each shapely syllable locked
    into the next,
        his lips stitched with certainty
        and even the roots
        of his tiny beard
        were crisped with context

What we heard
    we respected
        but the hole in his sock
        made us love him

(pale half moon of skin
    that fractured
    his innocent symmetry
        changing
        everything)

SINGER

Three-quarters drunk, late at night
across the subway platform, waiting
for the last train home, he swayed
serenely between two friends.

Their elbows dared
him, urging him forward
three lurching steps where he paused,
composed his hands and, self-appointed,
began to sing,

astonishing the air
with a crimson baritone, brandy-sweet,
touching us, touching even
the station roof with sound.

At the end
a Caruso bow and a bright
crack of applause
before the train came hurtling in.

From there we travelled across
the city while music unwound
to our destinations.
                    It stayed
with us carrying us on toward
the glittering transfer points,
humming in the final buses
to the veins of our jointed streets,
small as needles in the moonlight,
and still singing.

NEW POEMS

SUNDAY PAINTER

He comes early as an office worker, expectant
    but calm, unpacking precious pigment
    in the open air, an easel built
    like a crippled water bird, brushes, solvent
    and the self-forgetfulness that marks a dying breed,

but not quite, not quite; once he was told
    by a curious onlooker peering over his broad
    busy back that he was "good at clouds," and felt
    a spasm of joy or redemption or the blunt
    happiness of a man whose secret is at last revealed

and who afterwards is willing, endlessly, to invent
    on blank sky tinted blobs of cirrus and cumulus,
        pulled
    into white puffiness like wide-skirted brides
    walking through seasons, changes of government,
    conditions of health and family history,

and who, in the final few minutes of nearly spent
    light, busies himself with a quickly filled-
    in blue. "Cobalt," he announces to the clerestory
    of the closing day, his good sense briskly nailed
    down by that single word — *cobalt*

cobalt being the place where
    he lives, its blue stare
    and clarity his home address
    and refuge from nimbus glory,
    from imagination's uneasy shapelessness

SLEEPING

Children resist sleep
sensing its treachery
its false cycle

noticing how the elderly
relish their sleep

putting their old bones down
and pleasuring themselves
with their gassy lungs

They don't seem
to care where they happen to be
that they're not alone
or that their mouths sag open

or how they must creep
down the long cold slope
toward a familiar well-lit dream
that puffs and dissolves
into something as simple
as the next meal
or the pleasure of falling asleep
again

ACCIDENT

Curious journeys can be imagined
paper clips traveling inside a pocket
or burrs stuck to a sleeve
encircling the earth

If this is true
then why can't we believe
in the weight and worth
of accident, or that

the best of what we know
is randomly given
carried easily on difficult journeys
and lightly worn

BELIEVE ME

Believe me, there is no connection
between that man in the bus
station screaming in a foreign
language and the woman
sprawled on the roadway
crushed by a car

Most injuries are
separately born, believe me,
as accidental as that little star
we happen to notice
and then can't find again

CONFESSION

An anxious twitch of the nerves
    is all I get
    from sunsets, meadows, birds
    and all that

Mountains go flat
    on me and trees fall

but time's tenanted chronicle
    fills me full

REMEMBERING

You are remembering a drenching rain
    that fell last spring on the front lawn,
drumming the porch steps clean
    and scouring out the sad middle
of an afternoon

It was Sunday, a day made simple
    and slow by old routines
late rising, newspapers, heavy meals,
    hours sagging with their own dead weight,
that massed blue gloom of other Sundays
    and nothing to celebrate

until that sudden seizure
    of weather, one brimming half-hour
of beaten air
    and afterwards a glaze
of sunlight brighter than
    you could bear

WHENEVER

Whenever I look up
from my coffee or work
or whatever   it's sitting there

this crouching half-formed thing
like a crippled insect
scuttling in its legless way
at the edge of my eye
or coffee cup

its edges are sharp
reminding me
of its power to hurt
or be hurt

while sitting there
doing nothing

VOICES

At the museum certain
    objects
acquire a voice

the round porcelain
    humming, for instance,
of a Greek vase

or a Chinese lady's shoe
    screaming
in a glass case

JOURNEY

At Uncle Harvey's grave we can't stop grinning. The old
goat, we mutter affectionately, though God knows
why. He had a face bruised and broken with drink,
a missing leg and washed-up liver, and little else.

Beside him is Auntie Mae who liked to swank,
her rouge and nylons and dabs of cheap cologne.
Once she tapped his wrist and said, "Enough,"
at which he turned and punched her powdered nose.

Something about him larger and more vivid
keeps us freshly fond, the old bastard.
Something about her, unfocussed and ashamed,
reminds us why we came and what we are.

RELICS

Auntie Ruthie's fruited hat,
boat of truth
in a sea of right

Uncle Stanley's bamboo cane,
thin little wand
in a forest of fright

bodily relics burning alike
blackened holes
in a field of night

losing their shape
their name
their bite,

dying
particles
of light

FORTUNE

Our bad cousin could do
card tricks and headstands

He flunked St. Vincent's or got
thrown out we never knew

and married badly a girl
with crossed eyes who

died leaving him a dirty house
and four little kids,

the oldest who grew up to be
a doctor of divinity

and the second, a nurse
with the International Red Cross

and the next oldest, the mayor
of a medium-sized city

and the youngest, a tarot card reader
well known in the vicinity

and patronized by middle and upper-income clients
who swear by her astounding acuity

her starry predictions, her lucky guess
work, her steady gaze

her bare white arm stretched forward
fortune burning on every finger

AUNT VIOLET'S THINGS

Out of a book falls
a fluttery paper shape
1943 — pledging eternal
love, bordered with lace
sealed with symmetry
and on the back, sweet
sweet blandishments

Niggling parody
of that truer heart
infinitely more fragile
shy, misshapen and spent,
beating in its own rough cage
merely to keep time

THE INVENTION OF CLOCKS

First imagine history as a long dull night,
a drift of unlayered absence,
impacted, unknowable, profound until
that moment, a Sunday? (1274 some say,
guessing of course) when a young man
(probably) a sword-maker by trade
(here picture him as he may have been,
smallish and thoughtful and wearing
a coarse shirt and suffering — who knows —
from medieval angst, certainly boredom)
playing idly with an iron toy newly made
a thing of teased springs and wheels
and weights, queer marrying of metal parts
mathematics and foolishness — all
this so that whatever it is, that substance
that stands between the lifting and lowering
of his wife's hand (she is dropping turnips
into boiling water) can be measured
defined, possessed and offered back
to God who swings his musical old beard
like a pendulum

AT THE CLOCK MUSEUM

Something kingly
   in the quality brass, smoothed
   wood and quiet pedestal suggests
   a race of royal furniture
   dwarfish with faces and ticking throats

and fitted doll —
   neat doors   hinged and modest
   hiding nested springs, fine-toothed
   wheels, escapement, pendulum,
   weights, and always always a cheerful
   oily willingness to "keep" time

or at the very least to measure
   and record that insoluble
   other-water in which we float
   or sometimes   but rarely
     swim

NOW

Sunday night
moon chip

pollen   grit   ash   mote
grain of sand
speck of salt

seed and crumb
drum beat

silt from pocket
comma   dot
fear of nothing   kilowatt

tick tock   paint drop
dry like an atom
hard as thought

shock to the hand
catch in the throat
mid   night
day   break

QUARTZ

Quartz counts the hours now
so accurate, clean and quiet
that old Ma Greenwich could fall
down dead and never be missed

But cool moonly rituals
oddly persist,
their ironic minuet
of advancement and retreat
giving sly pleasure

and the words too —
equinox, solstice

CALENDAR NOTES

FLY PAN AM
the calendar trumpets

holidays circle
blink and bow

leap year squints
feints and conjures

mon thru sat
obedient children

sunday anarchy
violent red

twelve paper moons
ready to roll

GETTING

Getting
older we take
chances
with this useful love.

Like skaters turning
and pirouetting
on a winter lake
seen at a distance,

    we've been learning
    the double trick of balance
    and indifference

CARAGANA

That freak current of air reported on the news last week
was only spring approaching the western suburbs

First the parkland, then that long strip south
of the boulevard, then the chill rectangular yards

of brownish bungalows. Out of nothing, out
of knitted air, the caragana has sprung

to life, its leaves doubled and tripled
during the course of one thick muffled night

dreaming moisture from the moon, remembering sun
imagining tender lattices of light

establishing its tough dominion, spreading
truant through the fence, presumptuous, defiant

but keeping a deceptive feathery look
leggy, seductive, feminine, like

young girls in costume
dancing, foolish and compliant

SPRING

We're older this year
and as for spring we love
it less   violets, new leaves,
the tender unfolded air

mean not renewal but heaviness,
a coldness at the core,
like ourselves, honest, sober,
whom we also love less

COLD STORAGE

A month ago these same coats, capes, stoles
moved along cold springtime streets,
slipping into chilly cars, clutching at the last
spilled April accidents of weather

Wolverine, fox, beaver, mink
distinguished by quality and by dollars, by cut
(what's in this year, what's out),
by workmanship, size of pelt, genus,
species, family, coming down at last
to the creature itself (domestic or wild),
bones moving under fur,
blood, sensuality, a soul
some think, a brain of sorts, and instinct
which is — in the end — only a vast
unknowing, a muffled incomprehension
of itself, all split, sewn and styled
into seasons of new usefulness.

And now with stunning suddenness
they have been brought together.
Here flared exotic leopard meets
dyed rabbit: cleaned, bagged, insured, abandoned
to steep darkness, to plastic-swathed suspension.

Here machinery hums a perfect winter,
imposes hibernation from the wind and sun,
miles away from those natural/unnatural predators
lost to jointed memory, lost
under satin lining, sleeves and collars

so that the last feeble impulse is a giving
way to gravity, an unblinking absence
of that habit we call living,
a shut room, cleanliness, a season of silence.

TENTH REUNION

The evening itself dissolves

though later we regard
our photograph selves
pop-eyed with recall
mouths wild and scared
— *you're looking just the same!*

The camera brings resolve
and reason, a hard
focus on a bright wall,
the image that we came
here for, but can't afford

DAYLIGHT SAVING

The year is cut and spliced
at night   it's painless that way.

A Public Act   pragmatic but sound,
since the hour lost is practically free,
costs nothing   in fact,
and fits neatly   poetically
(you might say) in the hour found,

saving you sooner or later or   never
a stroke of cancelled grief or rapture,
more lustrous than the hardest coal
and loose   as mercury.

You could build a house there
in that hour   and a garden, shining
windows   flowers,
a high tight   fence,

or help yourself to a single moment,
randomly chosen   unproven   unfelt,
but sealed in a gel so pure
and white and weatherless,
you want to take it on your tongue,
to let it burn or melt
there   leaving behind its puzzling trace
its teasing fragrance.

HOUSE

Now that the house is officially listed
we like it less. Partly it's that
we're constrained by order, by the dusted
mouldings, touched-up paintwork and the flat
white untruthfulness of patched
over plaster. This is a house tuned
now to the better buyer, pitched
for the executive trade,
for those who want a pleasing address and a treed
lot, graciousness and, well, a certain
sense of, you know, tradition —
like birthdays and singing around the
piano and Sunday dinners, et cetera —
apportioned happiness waiting in the walls or
winking lewdly, grinning ear to ear

THE CLASS OF '53 — THIRTY YEARS LATER

Behind the photographs, under
the white faces stunned by light and
blinking back the dazzling arithmetic
of privilege, there we were,
composed and serious, and waiting for
the future to be revealed

as though the future had been bought
already like a solemn object
paid for by red roses and the white
of dresses, by dark suits and sealed
documents, by the false rhetoric
of the class poem, by nostalgia's inaccurate
and heartbreaking damage

There between Korea's tiny thunder
and the else and otherness of that much darker storm,
we waited for what was solid and calculable,
a sort of stamped and dated coinage
we could count and weigh or save
or possibly spend

And never this: this scarcely breathed-upon
mirror, whose long angled surface
bends with shifting colours,
of failed innocence and acts of grace,
of our scalding graffiti hearts,
our real estate, our marketplace,
our calm revisions, our sons and daughters,
our accident of health, our false alarms,
of accomplishment, love and language
in its hundred-thousand parts,
of words spoken on a windy night
or in a sunstruck room
and ourselves, gathered at the future's edge,
who still contrive by trickery or outrage
to take it in our arms.

WEDDING

The bride stands in white
fullness on the church steps
while cameras catch a mixed
show of joy and bafflement,
sunshine and blinked-back surprise
at the suddenly unfurled
afternoon of sentiment

and also the blue fixed
shock of hurt in her eyes
when she looks up and sees
storms of confetti hurled
with such precision, such fury that
she must freeze and ask herself what
it means and if it ever stops

HOLIDAY

Palm trees sudden as headaches
pop up, foolishly overlap
with leafless oaks
and poplars   bringing confusion

and we are uneasy about the sun,
loud bossy cousin
of the other sun

and can't quite cope
with the shock of our own
bare legs, so beggarly, so thin
like bony white orphans
we can't wait to abandon

FALLING BACK

It's easily done, spring and fall,
a dial turned or hands pushed and suddenly all
our lightly traced routines
    are differently lit —

Morning lopped
off, stone-cold and sharp with
crevasses, cutting harsh
    corners off yellow kitchens

But evenings yield,
grow soft, mouse-like, crushed
with fur, and cars
ascend greyed air
wave on wave, rising,
while children test their breath
    against emboldened light,

but cows in shadowed fields
scarcely move or lift
their heads
    and trees don't care

Seasons expand and shrink
    minutely

Planets cruise unstopped,
    their unaccompanied flight

FALL

This is the time of year when golden-agers
are taken on buses to view the autumn foliage
as though the sight and scent of yellowed trees
will stuff them with beautiful thoughts
and keep them from knowing —

as if there were still a trace of undamaged
hunger — for simple beauty, for colours,
the sun falling frail on the fret
work of every leaf, the trumpeting surprise
of the earth turning, returning.

Amazing the way they sit there oohing and ahhing,
behaving themselves and choking back their anger,
while non-stop movies play behind their eyes
scenes of unfiltered light
and focused rage —

God's handiwork, one of them piously announces —
and maybe when you get to be that age
you're willing to take the metaphors
you get, just to keep going:
dried sap, shrinkage, brittleness at the heart

or else the blind unthinking leverage
of custom, of perverse habit,
assembling around a summons to praise
what is fading, taking the corners
quietly, making the best of things

TOGETHER

Together so long
we've grown to look alike
   there's truth
   in these old myths

   You speak
   unrolling my own
   thoughts   breathe with
   half my breath

        at night we dream different
        dreams   but last night woke
        at the same instant
        as though an alarm
        had gone

WORK

All afternoon we stacked
wood against the garage.
It was hard work
made harder because
you were fractious and exact,
wanting neat terraced
rows of light and dark
while I would have put them any old way.

Afterwards we drank tea
and noticed how our hands shook
clumsy as paws
with the tiny cups,
as though the shock
of moving from brutal bark
to flowered china
had been too great

WALKERS

Walkers on a beach shiver
in sweaters   observe
the dull hinged sky   the flat glint
of pressed sand and vacant heavings

Then absence pulls together
the missing swimmers,
striped towels and picnic leavings and
prim sails from the summer nations

Shells crushed underfoot hint
at others carried home   rinsed
under city taps   set out on shelves
or on occasion lifted and turned
in winter hands

and praised for their calcium curves
the colour of harbours
their thin-edged forms
that hold the unnamed seasons
of else and other and there

SEASON'S GREETINGS

These crisp cards coming
out of nothing but
the reckoning of calendars

rattling through the door slot
fresh from aircraft and thrumming
with miles, their indistinct
messages scratched and signed
on the silvered backs of
angels and snow
scenes
      bringing not
knowledge or good cheer or love

but an eye blinked
backward at other richer
seasons, something more slender
than truth and more kind
      or less kind
than letting go